MICHEL ROUX

sauces for seafood

Dedication
To my son Alain, who cooks side-by-side with me at The Waterside Inn.

Contents

Foreword

The key to preparing a successful sauce for fish and shellfish is to follow a few very simple rules. Fish and shellfish are delicate creatures that inspire the creation of light sauces, rather modern in style, such as nages, beurre blanc, vegetable coulis and sabayons, as well as flavored butters, which melt gently over the flesh of poached or grilled fish.

You can use spirits, wine, fresh herbs, and spices in these sauces, but they must be used judiciously and parsimoniously so as not to mask the fine, delicate flavor and texture of the fish and shellfish. On the contrary, they should bring a harmony and subtlety to the seafood. It is vitally important to use only the freshest herbs and spices to ensure that you create a perfectly-balanced sauce.

My mother always used to say that the foods that come from the sea are among the tastiest, most tender and most natural. Fruits of the sea need only a very little sauce to enhance them without swamping them; any sauces for seafood need careful thought to achieve the perfect balance. When Maman prepared *moules marinières*, the aroma would waft out of the casserole, filling the air with the iodized scents of the sea. She only used shallots in this dish, never garlic, whose flavor she considered too aggressive for the delicate flesh of the little *bouchot* mussels.

On high days and holy days, the succulent mayonnaise she served with a cold poached codling was a treat for the palate. She could never understand why anyone needed to buy ready-made bottled mayonnaise. Holding her bowl with one hand and a fork in the other, she would rotate the fork in a precise circular movement, signaling with her eyes for me to drizzle in the oil in a thin trickle. In less than five minutes, the bowl was full of unctuous mayonnaise. As a reward for having helped her to make it, I was allowed to lick the fork..... Sometimes she added a few snipped leaves of tarragon, which she had bought in the market that very morning. She would place the herbs in a vase of water and keep them on the windowsill, just like a bunch of flowers. At The Waterside Inn, to bring pleasure to my customers, I have adopted the same principles of simplicity in my own approach to serving fish and shellfish.

I should like to remind my readers that there is no need to wash fish and shellfish in a lot of water, still less soak them for hours. It is enough to rinse them quickly under a trickle of cold water, then to dry them by dabbing delicately with a damp cloth. That way, you will preserve the firmness and texture of the flesh as well as the savor and aroma of this noble bounty from the sea.

About Sauces

In this book you will find sauces to suit every season, every taste, and every occasion. Some are modern, some classic, some light, others unctuous, depending on the fish and shellfish they are destined to accompany. All are creative, delicious and not difficult to make at home.

- All sauces, however simple or complex, should be based on good-quality ingredients. Aromatics, fresh herbs, spices, wines, spirits, stocks, and *fumets* must all be chosen with the utmost care.
- In sauce-making, balance is all-important. It is vital to get the proportions exactly right, particularly in sauces for fish and shellfish, whose delicate flavor must be allowed to shine through. A sauce should provide the perfect accompaniment to a dish, but it should never dominate it.
- Very strong-flavored ingredients like pungent spices, herbs, and alcohol should always be used in moderation.

Practical Advice

Menu Planning

If you plan to serve more than one sauce at a meal, make only one elaborate or rich sauce and keep the others light and simple. Avoid serving sauces of the same color and texture, and maintain a judicious balance between modern and classic sauces.

Techniques

Preparation time: The preparation times given in this book are based on ingredients that have already been measured and prepared as indicated in the ingredients list. They do not include the time taken to peel, chop, or slice vegetables or bones, soften butter, or any cooling time.

Cooking time: The timings given are only guidelines, since the degree of heat will vary depending on your stove and the type of saucepan used. The only infallible way to ensure that a sauce has reached the desired consistency is to check it on the back of a spoon.

Deglazing: Wine or stock is heated with the cooking juices and sediment left in the pan after pan-frying to make a sauce. Remove most of the fat or grease from the pan before adding the liquid.

Straining: Thin sauces can be passed straight through a conical sieve. Thicker sauces should be pushed through the sieve by pressing with the back of a ladle or twisting a small whisk.

Keeping sauces warm: A *bain-marie* is best for this. Use a saucepan large enough to hold the bowl containing the sauce, and fill the saucepan with hot water. Dot flakes of butter over the surface of white sauces to prevent a skin from forming.

Dairy Products

These play an extremely important part in sauce-making.

Crème fraîche: This can be heated to not more than 175°F, after which it will separate. To use it in a hot sauce, whisk it into the sauce off the heat without further cooking.

Heavy cream: This tolerates heat extremely well during cooking and can even be reduced by boiling. It is often used as a liaison, but above all makes sauces creamy and velvety.

Fromage blanc: This is the champion of low-calorie sauces and is available in both lowfat and nonfat versions. It is perfect for summer sauces, but its neutral taste demands the addition of flavorings like spices and herbs.

Hard cheeses: The most important and best are Parmesan, Gruyère, Emmenthal, and Cheddar. I always use freshly-grated medium-aged farmhouse cheeses, which have a delicious, full flavor. When adding cheese to a sauce, it takes a few minutes for the flavor to develop, so add it parsimoniously at first and check the development before adding more. Do not use cheap, poor-quality cheese, which can ruin a sauce by tasting rancid, soapy, or too salty.

Unsalted and clarified butter: I use only unsalted butter in my cooking; it is better for all sauces and essential for making clarified butter. To make about ½ cup clarified butter, gently melt 10 tablespoons unsalted butter and bring slowly to a boil. Skim off the froth, then pour the melted butter into a bowl, leaving behind the milky sediment in the pan.

Yogurt: I use tiny quantities of plain yogurt to add a touch of acidity to certain sauces for fish.

TO MAKE A BOUQUET GARNI
Wrap the herbs in the leek
leaf and tie up the bouquet
garni with string

A classic bouquet garni consists of a sprig of thyme, a bay leaf, parsley stems, and a leek leaf

Flavorings and Seasoning

Curry powder: A pinch of curry powder added to foaming butter will enhance the flavor of steamed fish.

Lemon and vinegar: A few drops of lemon juice or vinegar added to a characterless sauce just before serving will pep up the taste.

Saffron: To obtain the maximum flavor when using saffron threads, pound them in a mortar or crush them with your fingertips into the palm of your hand, then infuse them in a little warm water before using in recipes.

Salt and pepper: Never add too much salt to a sauce before it has reached the desired consistency and taste. Add pepper only just before serving to retain its flavor and zip.

Shallots: Shallots become bitter after chopping, so rinse them under cold water before using in a sauce.

Shellfish cooking juices: Keep the cooking juices from oysters, mussels, clams, etc. A soon as possible after cooking the mollusks, add a small amount of strained cooking liquor to fish sauces to reinforce their flavor and make them more complex.

Herbs and Spices

This subject deserves an entire encyclopaedia to do it justice, but since this is a book about sauces, I shall mention only those herbs and spices that I use to flavor and enhance my own cooking. If you use dried herbs, keep them in airtight jars in a cool, dark place. Spices lose their savor if they are kept too long; throw away any opened jars after 3–6 months because the spice will add nothing to your sauces, and may even spoil them.

Fines herbes: A mixture of fresh herbs in equal quantities: chervil, chives, parsley, and tarragon. They should be snipped, not chopped, only just before using so they retain the maximum flavor and do not become bitter.

The golden rules for using herbs and spices

• Go for quality rather than quantity when using herbs and spices; small quantities are usually enough.

• Do not mix contradictory and powerful flavors.

If you obey these rules, you will discover a wonderful world of flavors—subtle, complex, musky, fresh, spicy, and utterly delectable.

Vegetable Stock or Nage

Nages *are light, aromatic poaching stocks, and I like to add a hint of acidity to mine, hence the vinegar. I don't, however, use vinegar in my classic vegetable stock. You can substitute or add your own choice of seasonal vegetables, varying the stock with nice ripe tomatoes in summer, a few wild mushrooms in the fall (chanterelles add a particularly fine aroma), and so on.*

Ingredients:

3 carrots, cut in rounds

White part of 2 leeks, thinly sliced

2 celery stalks, thinly sliced

½ cup very thinly sliced bulb fennel

1 heaped cup thinly sliced shallots

⅔ cup thinly sliced onion

2 unpeeled garlic cloves

1 bouquet garni (page 9)

1 cup dry white wine

2 quarts water

3 tablespoons white wine vinegar (only for a nage)

10 white peppercorns, crushed and wrapped in a piece of cheesecloth

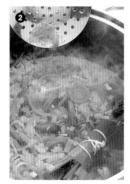

Makes 1½ quarts

Preparation time: 15 minutes

Cooking time: 45 minutes

Put all the ingredients except the peppercorns in a saucepan (1). Bring to a boil over high heat, then cook at a bare simmer for 45 minutes, skimming as necessary (2). After 35 minutes, add the cheesecloth-wrapped peppercorns. Strain through a fine-mesh conical sieve into a bowl (3). Cool the stock as quickly as possible (see below).

Cooling and freezing stocks

In the restaurant I cool my strained stocks very rapidly using a blast freezer to prevent the spread of bacteria. At home, I fill a container with ice cubes and plunge in the pan or bowl of boiling stock, which cools quite quickly. As soon as the stock is cold, I transfer it to airtight containers, keeping what I need in the refrigerator and freezing the rest. All stocks will keep in the refrigerator for several days, or in the freezer for up to 4 weeks.

❸

Fish Stock or Fumet

Fish stock can be used as the base for an aspic to serve with cold fish. Just add a little unflavored gelatin and season with salt and pepper before the gelatin sets. If you intend to use the stock for a red-wine sauce, substitute red wine for the white when making the stock.

Ingredients:

3¼ pounds bones and trimmings of white fish (e.g. sole, turbot, whiting), cut in pieces

4 tablespoons butter

White of 2 leeks, thinly sliced

½ cup thinly sliced onion

1 cup thinly sliced button mushrooms

1 cup dry white wine

1 bouquet garni (page 9)

2 slices of lemon

8 white peppercorns, crushed and wrapped in a piece of cheesecloth

Makes 2 quarts

Preparation time: *20 minutes*

Cooking time: *about 30 minutes*

Rinse the fish bones and trimmings under cold running water, then drain (1). In a saucepan, melt the butter and sweat the vegetables over low heat for a few minutes. Add the fish bones and trimmings (2), bubble gently for a few moments, and then pour in the wine (3). Cook until it has evaporated by two-thirds, then add 2½ quarts cold water (4). Bring to a boil, lower the heat, skim the surface (5), and add the bouquet garni and lemon. Simmer very gently for 25 minutes, skimming as necessary. 10 minutes before the end of cooking, add the cheesecloth-wrapped peppercorns (6). Gently ladle the stock through a fine-mesh conical sieve (7) and cool it as quickly as possible (see page 10).

Fish velouté: For an excellent fish *velouté*, add ¼ cup white roux (page 14) per quart of stock and cook for 20 minutes.

White Roux

This roux is classically used as a thickener in all white sauces.

Ingredients:	Makes just over ½ cup
6 tablespoons butter	Preparation time: *3 minutes*
½ cup flour	Cooking time: *4 minutes*

Melt the butter in a heavy-based saucepan. Off the heat, add the flour (1) and stir in with a small whisk or a wooden spoon (2). Cook over medium heat for 3 minutes, stirring continuously until a pale golden color (3). Transfer to a bowl, cover with plastic wrap, and keep at room temperature, or store in the refrigerator for several days.

Blond Roux

This pale roux is used to thicken veloutés and sauces where a neutral color is required, particularly those for white fish.

Ingredients:	Makes ½ cup
6 tablespoons butter	Preparation time: *3 minutes*
½ cup flour	Cooking time: *6 minutes*

Melt the butter in a heavy-based saucepan. Remove from the heat, add the flour (1), and stir in with a small whisk or a wooden spoon (2). Cook over medium heat for 5 minutes, stirring continuously until it becomes a pale hazelnut-brown (4). Transfer to a bowl, cover with plastic wrap, and keep at room temperature, or store in the refrigerator for several days.

Mayonnaise

Mayonnaise forms the basis for numerous other sauces. It is also delicious served just as it is with cold crab, lobster and shrimp, or poached fish such as salmon and cod; the list is endless.

If you prefer, you can replace some of the peanut oil with olive oil, but do not use more than one-quarter, because olive oil has a very pronounced flavor. For a creamier mayonnaise, mix in 2 tablespoons heavy cream after adding the warm vinegar or cold lemon juice.

Ingredients: *Serves 4*

2 egg yolks   *Preparation time: 5 minutes*

1 tablespoon strong Dijon mustard

1 cup peanut oil

1 tablespoon white wine vinegar, warmed, or 1 tablespoon cold lemon juice

Salt and freshly ground pepper

Lay a dish towel on the work surface and stand a mixing or salad bowl on the towel. In the bowl, combine the egg yolks, mustard, and a little salt and pepper, and mix with a whisk. Pour in the oil in a thin, steady stream, whisking continuously. When it is all incorporated, whisk more vigorously for 30 seconds to make a thick, glossy mayonnaise, then add the hot vinegar or cold lemon juice. Adjust the seasoning with salt and pepper.

The mayonnaise can be kept at room temperature, covered with plastic wrap, until ready to use. However, it is not wise to keep it for more than a few hours unless you use pasteurized eggs.

Mayonnaise makes a wonderful

dip for crustaceans

Recipes

- Sauces for fish should be delicate and light; their flavor should harmonize with the seafood they accompany and never dominate it. This is particularly important in the case of white fish. I like to serve fish with a *nage*, a light, aromatic stock, to which I sometimes add just a tiny *soupçon* of fresh herbs, like snipped chervil, basil, or tarragon.
- I prefer my fish barely cooked, so that it remains juicy. The sauce should be there to bring out the fresh, salty tang and the delicate flavor of the sea, adding extra pleasure to the palate.
- In contrast, sauces for crustaceans and mollusks should be flavored with stronger herbs and spices to give them a more defined edge and character.
- Sauces for fish and seafood often contain dry white wine; variations include beer, champagne, vermouth, or even a sweet Sauternes.

Tagliatelle and Seafood Sauce

with Saffron (page 28)

Fromage Blanc Sauce with Curry

Use this sauce as a dressing for a summer salad of green beans, new potatoes, or crudités, or with cold cooked mussels. You can adjust the quantity of curry slightly to suit your own taste, or even substitute ⅓ cup fresh mint, which you infuse in the milk. This version is delicious with cold pasta and a scattering of shredded mint leaves.

Ingredients:

½ cup milk

1 tablespoon curry powder

¾ pound (1½ cups) fromage blanc

(whichever fat content you prefer)

Salt and freshly ground pepper

Serves 6

Preparation time: 3 minutes

Cooking time: 2 minutes, plus cooling

In a small saucepan, bring the milk to a boil. Add the curry, simmer for 2 minutes, then leave at room temperature to cool completely. Strain the cold curry-flavored milk through a wire-mesh sieve, then stir it into the *fromage blanc*. Season to taste with salt and pepper. The sauce is now ready to use.

Yogurt Sauce

This simple, refreshing sauce is excellent with all cold vegetables, cold pasta, and hard-boiled eggs as well as with fish. It is very quick to make.

Ingredients:

2½ cups plain yogurt

½ cup mayonnaise (see page 15)

2 tablespoons snipped fresh herbs of
your choice (e.g. chervil,
parsley, chives, tarragon)

1 medium tomato, peeled
(page 34), seeded, and diced

A small pinch of cayenne,
or 4 drops of hot-pepper sauce

Salt

Serves 8

Preparation time: 10 minutes

Mix all the ingredients together and, *voilà*, your sauce is ready to serve.

Fresh Goat-Cheese Sauce with Rosemary

Serve this sauce with a basket of crudités, *cold poached fish, roast or poached chicken, or with large pink shrimp.*

Ingredients:

1 cup milk (if the cheese has a very soft consistency, you may need only ⅔–¾ cup)

¼ cup fresh rosemary needles

¾ pound fresh goat cheese, softened with a spatula

Salt and freshly ground pepper

Serves 6

Preparation time: 3 minutes

Cooking time: 2 minutes, plus cooling

In a small saucepan, bring the milk to a boil. Add the rosemary needles, cover the pan, and leave to infuse until completely cold. Strain the cooled milk, whisk it into the goat cheese, and season to taste with salt and pepper. The sauce is now ready to serve.

Fishbone Sauce

This sauce is quick to prepare, light, and full of flavor. It goes very well with poached fish or steamed scallops.

Ingredients:

10 tablespoons butter, diced

⅓ cup chopped shallot

½ pound white fish bones (e.g. sole or turbot), roughly chopped

½ cup dry white wine

½ cup cold water

1 sprig of thyme

A few drops of lemon juice

Salt and freshly ground pepper

Serves 4

Preparation time: 10 minutes

Cooking time: 10 minutes

Melt 4 tablespoons butter in a small saucepan. Add the shallot and fish bones, and sweat gently for 3 minutes, stirring with a wooden spoon.. Pour in the wine and cook for 2 minutes. Add the water and thyme and bubble for 3 minutes, then skim the surface if necessary. Toss in the remaining butter, one piece at a time, rotating the pan and swirling it about to incorporate the butter, then add the lemon juice. Season to taste with salt and pepper, and pass the sauce through a wire-mesh conical sieve. It is now ready to use.

Asparagus Coulis

This delicious sauce is almost as light as a nage. *I add some asparagus tips at the last moment and serve it with delicate steamed fish, or pour it around my vegetable lasagne to make a dish that even non-vegetarians love.*

Ingredients:

¾ pound asparagus spears, preferably small ones

4 tablespoons butter

⅔ cup chopped shallots

1 sprig of thyme

1¼ cups Vegetable Stock (page 10), chicken stock, or water

2 cups heavy cream

1 teaspoon soy sauce (optional)

Salt and freshly ground pepper

Serves 8

Preparation time: **10 minutes**

Cooking time: **about 40 minutes**

Peel the asparagus stalks with a vegetable peeler. Cut off the tips and blanch them in boiling salted water. Refresh, drain, and set aside. Chop the stalks and leave them raw. In a thick-bottomed saucepan, melt the butter, add the chopped asparagus stalks and shallot, and sweat gently for 5 minutes. Add the thyme and the stock or water, and cook over medium heat for 15 minutes. Pour in the cream, increase the heat to high, and reduce the coulis by one-third. Whizz in a blender for 3 minutes, then pass through a conical sieve. Season to taste, adding the reserved asparagus tips and the soy sauce if you wish. Keep the coulis warm until needed.

Light Carrot Coulis

This coulis is almost like a jus *and should be eaten with a spoon. It goes well with pan-fried scallops, grilled white fish, and also with rice pilaff.*

Ingredients:

3 carrots, total weight about ½ pound

Juice of 2 oranges

1 cup Vegetable Stock (page 10) or veal stock

1 teaspoon freshly grated ginger

4 tablespoons butter, chilled and diced

Salt and freshly ground pepper

Serves 6

Preparation time: **5 minutes**

Cooking time: **about 10 minutes**

Peel the carrots, cut them into small pieces, then whizz them in a food processor with the orange juice and stock for 3 minutes. Transfer to a saucepan, set over high heat, and reduce the coulis for about 10 minutes, until it lightly coats the back of a spoon. Add the ginger, take the pan off the heat, and whisk in the butter, a little at a time. Season to taste, pass through a conical sieve, and serve.

Leek Coulis with Curry

Spread a spoonful of this coulis over individual plates and top with grilled or pan-fried firm-fleshed fish such as monkfish or turbot, or some shrimp à la meunière.

Ingredients:

1 pound tender small or medium leeks

3 tablespoons butter

½ tsp curry powder

1 cup Vegetable Stock (page 10)
or chicken stock

1¼ cups heavy cream

½ teaspoon mustard powder

Salt and freshly ground pepper

Serves 8

Preparation time: **10 minutes**

Cooking time: **about 40 minutes**

Cut off the greenest parts of the leeks and the root ends. Split the leeks lengthwise, wash meticulously in cold water, and slice them finely. Blanch in boiling salted water, refresh, and drain.

In a thick-bottomed saucepan, melt the butter and sweat the leeks gently for 10 minutes. Add the curry powder, then the stock, and cook over medium heat for 10 minutes. Add the cream and mustard powder and simmer for 10 minutes longer, then whizz in a blender for 5 minutes. Pass the coulis through a conical sieve back into the pan. Season and keep the coulis warm, without letting it boil, until ready to serve.

Shrimp Butter

Pats of shrimp butter add a special something to pan-fried or grilled fish. It can be used to enrich a fish sauce, or served spread on toasted croûtons to make canapés. For extra zing, add a pinch of cayenne.

Ingredients:

5 ounces very fresh cooked shrimp

10 tablespoons butter, softened

Cayenne (optional)

Makes about 1 cup

Preparation time: 10 minutes

Rinse the shrimp in cold water, leaving any eggs attached, drain, and pat dry in a dish towel.

Place the shrimp in a blender with the butter and a pinch of cayenne, if you like (1). Process for about 3 minutes, scraping the ingredients into the center of the bowl every minute, to obtain a homogeneous mixture (2). If you prefer, you can use a pestle and mortar instead of a blender.

Using a plastic scraper, rub the flavored butter through a drum sieve to eliminate the shrimp shells (3). Using plastic wrap, roll the butter into one or two sausage shapes, and refrigerate or freeze until ready to slice and serve.

Pan-fried fish topped with Shrimp Butter

Langoustine Butter

Enrich fish sauces with this butter. It also makes wonderful canapés spread on toast croûtons and topped with prawns or shrimp.

Ingredients:

4 tablespoons butter, preferably clarified (page 8)

1 small carrot, finely diced

1 medium onion, finely diced

12 langoustines (Dublin Bay prawns), or crayfish, live if possible

5 tablespoons cognac or Armagnac

1 cup white wine

1 small bouquet garni (page 9)

2 pinches of cayenne

Softened butter, 75% of the weight of the cooked crustacean heads and claws

Salt and freshly ground pepper

Makes about 2 cups

Preparation time: **15 minutes**

Cooking time: **about 20 minutes**

Melt the butter in a deep frying pan, add the diced carrot and onion, and sweat until soft. Using a slotted spoon, transfer the vegetables to a bowl, leaving the cooking butter in the pan.

Put the crustaceans in the pan and sauté over high heat for 2 minutes. Add the cognac, ignite it, and then moisten with the white wine. Add the cooked diced vegetables, bouquet garni, a little cayenne, and a small pinch of salt. Cook gently over low heat for 10 minutes. Tip all the contents of the pan into a bowl and leave to cool completely at room temperature.

To make the flavored butter, separate the prawn or crayfish heads and tails. Keep the tails for another use (as an hors d'oeuvre salad or canapés, for example). Gather up the heads and claws, and the creamy flesh ("butter") from the heads, and weigh them. Put them in a food processor or blender with 75% of their weight of softened butter and the diced vegetables, and whizz until mushy. Using a plastic scraper, rub through a drum sieve and season to taste. Using plastic wrap, roll the flavored butter into one or two sausage shapes, and refrigerate or freeze until needed.

Pistachio Butter

I use this butter in my Sauternes Sauce with Pistachios (page 44) or add it to a hollandaise (page 49) to give a touch of mellowness.

Ingredients:

¾ cup skinned pistachio nuts

1 tablespoon water

10 tablespoons butter, softened

Salt and freshly ground pepper

Makes about 1 cup

Preparation time: 7 minutes

Pound the pistachios to a paste with the water in a mortar or food processor. Add all the butter at once, mix, and season, then rub through a drum sieve with a plastic scraper. Using plastic wrap, roll the pistachio butter into one or two sausage shapes, and refrigerate or freeze until ready to use.

Anchovy Butter

Use this delicious butter on grilled fish, or serve it on toast canapés topped with a julienne *of anchovy fillets.*

Ingredients:

2 ounces anchovy fillets in oil

10 tablespoons butter, softened

Salt and freshly ground pepper

Makes about ¾ cup

Preparation time: 7 minutes

Chop the anchovy fillets or pound them in a mortar. Using a wooden spoon, mix them into the butter and, using a plastic scraper, rub through a drum sieve or whizz in a food processor. Season, being circumspect with the salt because the anchovies already contain plenty. Use plastic wrap to roll the butter into one or two sausage shapes, and refrigerate or freeze until ready to use.

Crustacean Oil

This wonderfully delicate oil is one of my favorites. It makes a superb dressing for fantasy seafood salads or warm asparagus spears.

Ingredients:

2¼ pounds langoustines (Dublin Bay prawns) or crayfish, cooked in salted water

½ head of garlic, unpeeled

1 sprig of thyme

2 bay leaves

1 small bunch of tarragon

1 teaspoon whole white peppercorns

½ teaspoon whole coriander seeds

Approximately 1 quart peanut or olive oil

Salt

Special equipment:

A 1-quart canning jar. Ideally, this should be new—if not, it must be scrupulously clean

Makes about 1 quart

Preparation time: 20 minutes, plus 3 hours' drying

Sterilization time: 35–45 minutes

Preheat the oven to 250°F. Remove the eyes of the crustaceans, and separate the heads, claws, and tails (1). Keep the tails to use as a garnish for fish or serve in a salad as an hors d'oeuvre. Roughly chop the heads and claws with a chef's knife (2), put them in a roasting pan, and place in the oven to dry for 3 hours. Put the dried heads and claws into the canning jar with the aromatics, fill up with oil to within 1 inch of the top (3), and seal the lid carefully.

To sterilize the oil, you will need a pan at least as tall as the jar. Line the bottom and sides of the pan with foil; this will protect the glass, which might explode if it should knock against the side of the pan. Put in the jar (4) and pour in enough water, salted with 1 cup salt per quart of water, to come up to the level of the oil in the jar, but not to submerge it. Bring the water to a boil over high heat and boil for 35–45 minutes, depending on the size of the jar.

After sterilization, leave the jar at room temperature until completely cold, then refrigerate for at least 8 days before using the oil. It will keep for months in the sealed sterile jar if stored in a cool place. Once opened, decant the oil into a bottle; it will keep for several weeks in the refrigerator.

Seafood Sauce with Saffron

This is the perfect sauce for any lightly poached seafood, for jumbo shrimp or lobster, or for fresh flat pasta (picture page 16).

Ingredients:

1½ cups cooking juices from shellfish, such as mussels, scallops, oysters, clams, etc

1 cup Fish Stock (page 13), or cooking juices from shrimp or lobster

A pinch of saffron threads

1 cup heavy cream

Salt and freshly ground white pepper

Serves 4

Preparation time: **10 minutes**

Cooking time: **about 20 minutes**

Combine the shellfish juices and fish stock in a saucepan, set over high heat, and reduce by two-thirds. Add the saffron and cream and bubble for 5 minutes, until the sauce will lightly coat the back of a spoon. Pass it through a conical sieve and season to taste. For a less calorific sauce, you can substitute fromage blanc for the heavy cream, but do not allow the sauce to boil. Heat it to 195°F and whisk well before serving, or, better still, give it a quick whizz in a blender.

Champagne Sauce

This sauce is perfect for poached white fish, such as John Dory, turbot, or sole. You can substitute sparkling white wine for the champagne, but the sauce will not taste as good.

Ingredients:

4 tablespoons butter

½ cup very finely sliced shallots

¾ cup finely sliced button mushrooms

1¾ cups brut champagne

1¼ cups Fish Stock (page 13)

2 cups heavy cream

Salt and freshly ground white pepper

Serves 8

Preparation time: **10 minutes**

Cooking time: **about 50 minutes**

In a saucepan, melt 1½ tablespoons butter. Add the shallots and sweat them for 1 minute, without coloring. Add the mushrooms and cook for 2 minutes longer, stirring continuously with a wooden spatula. Pour in the champagne and reduce by one-third over medium heat. Add the fish stock and reduce the sauce by half.

Pour in the cream and reduce the sauce until it lightly coats the back of a spoon. Pass it through a fine-mesh conical sieve into a clean pan. Whisk in the remaining butter, a little at a time, then season the sauce with salt and pepper. For a lighter texture, whizz the sauce in a food processor for 1 minute before serving.

Nantua Sauce

An excellent sauce for large shrimp, scallops, and any white fish with delicate, firm flesh. A tablespoon of snipped tarragon added just before serving will make the sauce taste even better.

Ingredients:

½ cup butter

½ cup very finely sliced shallots

¾ cup very finely sliced button mushrooms

16 crayfish or langoustine *(Dublin Bay prawn) heads, raw or cooked, roughly chopped*

2 tablespoons cognac

⅔ cup dry white wine

1¼ cups Fish Stock (page 13)

1 small bouquet garni (page 9), including a sprig or two of tarragon

½ cup chopped ripe tomatoes, peeled (page 34) and seeded

A pinch of cayenne

1¼ cups heavy cream

Salt and freshly ground pepper

Serves 8

Preparation time: **20 minutes**

Cooking time: **about 50 minutes**

In a shallow saucepan, melt 3 tablespoons butter over low heat. Add the shallots and mushrooms and sweat for 1 minute. Add the crayfish or prawn heads to the pan, increase the heat, and fry briskly for 2–3 minutes, stirring continuously with a spatula.

Pour in the cognac, and ignite with a match. Add the wine and reduce by half, then pour in the fish stock. Bring to a boil, then lower the heat so that the sauce bubbles gently. Add the bouquet garni, tomatoes, cayenne, and a bit of salt and cook for 30 minutes.

Stir in the cream and bubble the sauce for 10 minutes longer. Remove the bouquet garni, transfer the contents of the pan to a food processor, and whizz for 2 minutes. Strain the sauce through a fine-mesh conical sieve into a clean saucepan, rubbing it through with the back of a ladle. Bring the sauce back to a boil and season with salt and pepper. Off the heat, whisk in the remaining butter, a little at a time, until the sauce is smooth and glossy. It is now ready to serve.

Américaine Sauce

This classic "star" takes time to prepare, but is worth the effort. Serve it with firm-fleshed fish, such as poached turbot.

Serves 6

Preparation time: 40 minutes

Cooking time: about 1 hour

Ingredients:

1 live lobster, 1¾—2 pounds

A small pinch of cayenne

½ cup peanut oil

⅓ cup very finely diced carrots

3 tablespoons very finely diced shallot or onion

2 garlic cloves, unpeeled and crushed

¼ cup cognac or Armagnac

1¼ cups dry white wine

1¼ cups Fish Stock (page 13)

½ pound very ripe tomatoes, peeled (page 34), seeded, and chopped (1½ cups)

1 bouquet garni (page 9), containing a sprig of tarragon

4½ tablespoons butter

1½ tablespoons flour

⅓ cup heavy cream (optional)

Salt and freshly ground pepper

Bring a large pan of water to a boil. Rinse the lobster under cold running water and plunge it into boiling water for 45 seconds. Separate the head and body, and cut the claw joints and tail into rings across the articulations (1). Split the head lengthwise, remove the gritty sac close to the feelers (2), and the dirty white membranes. Scrape out the greenish coral (tomalley) from inside the head (3) and reserve in a bowl. Season the lobster with cayenne, salt, and pepper.

In a deep frying pan or shallow saucepan, heat the oil over high heat. As soon as it is sizzling hot, add all the lobster pieces (4) and sauté until the shell turns bright red and the flesh is lightly colored (5). Remove the lobster pieces with a slotted spoon (6) and place on a plate. Discard most of the cooking oil.

Using the same pan, sweat the carrot and shallot until soft but not colored. Add the garlic, return the

lobster pieces to the pan, pour in the cognac or Armagnac, and light with a match. Add the wine and fish stock, then add the tomatoes, bouquet garni, and a touch of salt. As soon as the mixture comes to a boil, lower the heat and cook gently for 15 minutes. Remove and reserve the claws and rings of lobster tail containing the meat. Cook the sauce at a gentle bubble for 30 minutes longer, skimming it every 15 minutes.

Using a fork, mash together the reserved lobster coral, butter, and flour, and add this mixture to the sauce, a little at a time (7). Cook for 5 minutes longer, then add the cream if desired and pass the sauce through a fine-mesh conical strainer, pressing it through with the back of a ladle (8). Season with salt and pepper. For a lighter texture, whizz the sauce in a food processor for 1 minute. Remove the reserved lobster meat from the shell, dice it and add to the sauce just before serving.

Red-Wine Sauce

Serve this vinous, characterful sauce as a base for thin slices (scallops) of pan-fried pink-fleshed fish, such as salmon or tuna. For a fuller flavor, use 1 cup veal stock and 1¼ cups fish stock.

Ingredients:

1¼ cups full-bodied red wine

2¼ cups Fish Stock (page 13), made with red wine

⅓ cup finely sliced shallots

¾ cup finely sliced button mushrooms

1 small bouquet garni (page 9)

¼ cup heavy cream

14 tablespoons butter, chilled and diced

Salt and freshly ground pepper

Serves 8

Preparation time: **5 minutes**

Cooking time: **about 40 minutes**

Combine all the ingredients except the cream and butter in a saucepan, set over medium heat, and reduce until slightly syrupy. Remove the bouquet garni, add the cream, and give the sauce a good bubble, then strain it through a conical sieve into a clean saucepan. Whisk in the butter, a small piece at a time, until the sauce is rich and glossy. Season to taste and serve hot.

Bercy Sauce

This simple, classic sauce goes well with any red- or white-fleshed fish. I enjoy it served with an unusual fish, roussette *(which is a kind of shark), and also with skate.*

Ingredients:

4 tablespoons butter

½ cup minced shallots

1 cup dry white wine

⅔ cup Fish Stock (page 13)

1¾ cups Fish Velouté (page 13)

Juice of ½ lemon

2 tablespoons chopped parsley, or 1 tablespoon snipped tarragon

Salt and freshly ground pepper

Serves 6

Preparation time: **10 minutes**

Cooking time: **about 35 minutes**

Melt 1½ tablespoons butter in a saucepan, add the minced shallots, and sweat them gently for 1 minute. Pour in the wine and fish stock and cook over medium heat until the liquid has reduced by half. Add the fish *velouté* and simmer gently for 20 minutes. The sauce should be thick enough to coat the back of a spoon lightly. If it is not, cook it for 5–10 minutes longer. Remove from the heat and whisk in the remaining butter and the lemon juice. Season the sauce, stir in the chopped parsley or tarragon, and serve immediately.

Tomato Nage

This light nage *is perfect with lightly poached shellfish, or grilled fish such as slices of salmon or fillets of sole.*

Ingredients:

¾ pound very ripe tomatoes, peeled
(page 34), seeded, and chopped (2 cups)
⅓ cup finely sliced shallots
⅔ cup finely sliced button mushrooms
1 sprig of thyme
1 bay leaf
1 cup Vegetable Stock (page 10)
A pinch of sugar
¼ cup heavy cream
1 cup butter
1 teaspoon tomato paste (optional)
Salt and freshly ground pepper

Serves 8
Preparation time: 15 minutes
Cooking time: 25 minutes

Combine all the ingredients except the cream and butter in a saucepan and bring to a boil over medium heat. As soon as the mixture starts to bubble, lower the heat and reduce the liquid by two-thirds. Now add the cream and bubble the sauce for 3 minutes. Off the heat, whisk in the butter, a little at a time. Strain the sauce through a fine-mesh conical sieve into a clean saucepan and season to taste. The *nage* is now ready to use.

If the tomatoes are slightly lacking in flavor, add a teaspoon of tomato paste.

Fish Fumet with Tomatoes

This summery, fat-free sauce is delicious ladled over steamed fillets of fish such as John Dory, sole, or bream (porgy).

Ingredients:

2½ cups Fish Stock (page 13)
1 pound very ripe tomatoes, chopped
1 small red bell pepper, white membranes
and seeds removed, very thinly sliced
1 heaped cup basil, coarsely chopped
4 egg whites
8 peppercorns, crushed
Salt and freshly ground pepper

Serves 6
Preparation time: 5 minutes
Cooking time: about 30 minutes

First make the clarification mixture, which will make the *fumet* crystal-clear. Thoroughly mix together all the ingredients except the fish stock. Pour the fish stock into a saucepan and add the clarification mixture. Bring to a boil over medium heat, stirring every 5 minutes with a wooden spoon. As soon as the liquid boils, reduce the heat and bubble very gently for 20 minutes. Pass the clarified *fumet* through a wire-mesh conical sieve, season with salt and pepper, and serve.

How to peel tomatoes: Cut a cross in the top of the tomatoes and gouge out the cores. Drop the tomatoes into boiling water until the skin starts to split (about 10–20 seconds), then take them out and plunge them into ice water. Lift out the tomatoes with a draining spoon and slip off the skins.

Cooked Tomato Coulis

This tomato coulis is extremely versatile, and I use it frequently in my kitchen. It is divine spread over a plate and topped with grilled fish. Alternatively add a small quantity to a fish sauce or, better still, a béchamel (page 58).

Serves 4
Preparation time: 5 minutes
Cooking time: about 1 hour

Ingredients:

⅔ cup olive oil
2 garlic cloves, crushed
⅓ cup minced shallots
1 small bouquet garni (page 9), containing plenty of thyme
1½ pounds very ripe tomatoes, peeled (opposite), seeded, and chopped
1 tablespoon tomato paste (only if the tomatoes are not ripe enough)
A pinch of sugar
6 peppercorns, crushed
Salt

In a thick-bottomed saucepan, warm the olive oil with the garlic, shallot, and bouquet garni. After 2 minutes, add the tomatoes (1), tomato paste if needed, sugar, and crushed peppercorns. Cook very gently for about 1 hour, stirring occasionally with a wooden spoon until all the moisture has evaporated (2). Remove the bouquet garni and whizz the contents of the pan in a blender to make a smooth purée (3). Season to taste. The coulis is ready to use immediately, but you can keep it in an airtight container in the refrigerator for 5 days.

If the sauce is to be served plain, after reheating, add a little olive oil just before serving.

Mandarin Sauce

This sauce glows with color and warmth and is particularly good in fall or winter. Its delicious gentle flavor makes it ideal with poached white-fleshed fish. I serve it with paupiettes of sole, simply poached or filled with a lobster mousse.

Serves 4

Preparation time: 7 minutes

Cooking time: about 20 minutes

Ingredients:

1½ cups peeled mandarin or tangerine sections

⅔ cup Fish Stock (page 13)

⅔ cup heavy cream

2 tablespoons Napoleon mandarine liqueur or Grand Marnier

4 tablespoons butter, chilled and diced

Zest of 1 mandarin or tangerine, cut in julienne and blanched (optional)

Salt and freshly ground pepper

Put the mandarin sections in a food processor, mix to a pulp, and rub through a fine-mesh sieve. Pour the resulting mandarin juice and the fish stock into a small saucepan, set over medium heat, and reduce by half. Add the cream and liqueur and bubble the sauce for a few minutes, until it lightly coats the back of a spoon. Pass it again through the conical sieve. Off the heat, whisk in the butter, a little at a time, to make a smooth, shiny sauce. Season to taste, then add the mandarin zest if you wish. Serve at once.

Paupiettes of sole filled with lobster mousse, served with Mandarin Sauce

Parsley Nage with Lemon Grass

This light, fresh sauce has a gentle lemony flavor underlying the delicious aroma of parsley. Serve it with any poached or pan-fried fish, or with scallops and jumbo shrimp.

Ingredients:

2 cups flat-leaf parsley, stems and leaves coarsely chopped

¼ cup chopped shallot

1 lemon grass stalk, split lengthwise

1¼ cups Fish Stock (page 13) or Vegetable Stock (page 10)

¼ cup heavy cream

Juice of ½ lemon

14 tablespoons butter, chilled and diced

2 tablespoons finely snipped parsley leaves

Salt and freshly ground pepper

Serves 6

Preparation time: **10 minutes**

Cooking time: **about 30 minutes**

Put the chopped parsley, shallot, lemon grass, and stock in a saucepan and cook very gently for 10 minutes. Remove the lemon grass, transfer the contents of the pan to a blender, and purée for 1 minute. Pass the purée through a wire-mesh conical sieve into a clean saucepan, add the cream and lemon juice, and bring to a boil. Bubble until the sauce is just thick enough to coat the back of a spoon very lightly. Reduce the heat to as low as possible and incorporate the butter, a little at a time, whisking continuously. Season the sauce to taste with salt and pepper, stir in the finely snipped parsley, and serve at once.

Watercress Sauce

A tasty sauce to serve with grilled scallops or lightly poached oysters. It is extremely light, almost like a bouillon, and should be eaten with a spoon.

Ingredients:

just under 1 pound very green watercress

7 tablespoons butter

2 cups Vegetable Stock (page 10)

2 tablespoons soft green peppercorns

Salt and freshly ground pepper

Serves 8

Preparation time: **about 25 minutes**

Cooking time: **about 25 minutes**

Cut off and discard most of the watercress stems. In a saucepan, melt 2 tablespoons of the butter. Add the watercress and sweat it over low heat for 3 minutes, stirring continuously with a spatula.

Add the vegetable stock and green peppercorns, increase the heat to high, and cook for 10 minutes. Remove from the heat and leave the sauce to infuse for 10 minutes, then pour it into a food processor and whizz for 2 minutes. Pass the sauce through a fine-mesh conical sieve into a clean saucepan, rubbing it through with the back of a ladle. Reheat until bubbling, then take the pan off the heat and whisk in the remaining butter, a little at a time. Season with salt and pepper.

Thermidor Sauce

This famous companion to lobster thermidor is sadly often poorly made and therefore disappointing. I enjoy it with almost all shellfish, especially mixed with crabmeat and served au gratin. If you wish, add a teaspoon of cognac to the sauce at the end of cooking.

Ingredients:

⅓ cup minced shallots

1 cup Fish Stock (page 13)

1 cup dry white wine

1¼ cups Béchamel Sauce (page 58)

½ cup heavy cream

1 teaspoon strong Dijon mustard

1 teaspoon English mustard powder, dissolved in a few drops of water

4 tablespoons butter, chilled and diced

1 tablespoon finely snipped tarragon

Salt and cayenne

Serves 6

Preparation time: *10 minutes*

Cooking time: *about 40 minutes*

Combine the shallots, fish stock, and wine in a saucepan and reduce the liquid by two-thirds. Add the béchamel and cook the sauce over low heat for 20 minutes, stirring every 5 minutes. Pour in the cream, bubble for 5 minutes, then add both mustards and cook for 2 minutes longer. Remove from the heat and whisk the butter into the sauce, one piece at a time. Season with salt and a large pinch of cayenne. Finally, add the tarragon and serve immediately.

Curried Mussel Sauce

This sauce accompanies to perfection mussels cooked à la marinière *and taken out of their shells, or poached cod or halibut. It is also wonderful with a rice pilaff or a dish of pasta bows.*

Serves 6
Preparation time: 5 minutes
Cooking time: about 25 minutes

Ingredients:
4 tablespoons butter
⅓ cup minced onion
1 tablespoon curry powder
2 tablespoons flour
2 cups cooking juices from mussels and other shellfish, such as clams
1 small bouquet garni (page 9)
⅔ cup heavy cream
Salt and freshly ground pepper

Melt the butter in a saucepan, add the onions, and sweat over low heat for 3 minutes. Add the curry powder (1) and flour (2), stir with a wooden spoon, and cook for another 3 minutes, then pour in the cold shellfish juices. Put in the bouquet garni, bring to a boil, and leave the sauce to bubble very gently for 20 minutes, stirring with the wooden spoon every 5 minutes. Add the cream (3), give another bubble, then discard the bouquet garni and season the sauce with salt and pepper. Serve immediately.

Curried Mussel Sauce can be made with the juices from other shellfish, such as clams

Shrimp Sauce

This is delicious with almost all poached, steamed, or braised fish. I also love it poured over quartered hard-boiled eggs. I sometimes add a couple of tablespoons of dry sherry to the sauce just before serving.

Ingredients:

3 tablespoons Blond Roux, hot (page 14)

2½ cups Fish Stock, cooled (page 13)

1 cup heavy cream

4 tablespoons Shrimp Butter (page 23)

½ cup cooked and peeled small shrimp

A pinch of cayenne

Salt and freshly ground pepper

Serves 6

Preparation time: **15 minutes**

Cooking time: **about 45 minutes**

Put the hot roux in a saucepan, set over medium heat, and whisk in the cold fish stock. As soon as it comes to a boil, reduce the heat to very low and cook gently for 30 minutes, whisking every 10 minutes and making sure that the whisk goes right into the bottom of the pan. Use a spoon to remove any skin that forms on this *velouté* as it cooks.

After 30 minutes, add the cream and bubble the sauce for 10 minutes longer. Reduce the heat to the lowest possible (use a heat diffuser if you have one) and whisk in the shrimp butter, a little at a time. Season the sauce with salt and pepper and spice it up with cayenne to taste. Pass it through a wire-mesh conical sieve, then add the shrimp and serve immediately.

Mango Sauce

This refreshing, fruity sauce is perfect for outdoor eating in summer. It is excellent with grilled or fish or with crustaceans such as lobster or jumbo shrimp.

Ingredients:

1 mango, about ½ pound

¼ cup cognac or Armagnac

A small pinch of curry powder

1 tablespoon soft green peppercorns, well drained

1¼ cups Fish Stock (page 13)

1 cup heavy cream

½ cup plain yogurt

1 tablespoon snipped flat-leaf parsley

Salt and freshly ground pepper

Serves 6

*Preparation time: **10 minutes***

*Cooking time: **about 40 minutes***

Using a knife with a fine blade, peel the mango and cut away the flesh from around the pit. Put the flesh in a saucepan with the cognac or Armagnac, curry, and green peppercorns and simmer over low heat for 5 minutes. Pour in the fish stock and bubble gently for 20 minutes. Add the cream and cook for 5 minutes longer, then remove from the heat and add the yogurt. Transfer the sauce to a blender and whizz for 30 seconds, then pass it through a wire-mesh conical sieve and season to taste with salt and pepper. Serve the sauce immediately, or keep it warm (but not too hot) in a *bain-marie*. Stir in the parsley just before serving.

Sauternes Sauce with Pistachios

I like to serve this sauce with poached or steamed fillets of sole, salmon, sea bass, or turbot. Depending on the fish, I sometimes add some freshly skinned and chopped pistachios to the sauce just before serving.

Ingredients:

1½ tablespoons butter

2 cups thinly sliced button mushrooms

1¼ cups sweet white wine (Sauternes or Barsac)

2½ cups Fish Stock (page 13)

⅓ cup Blond Roux (page 14), cooled

⅔ cup heavy cream

⅓ cup Pistachio Butter (page 25)

Salt and freshly ground pepper

Serves 6

*Preparation time: **10 minutes***

*Cooking time: **about 40 minutes***

Melt the butter in a saucepan, add the mushrooms, and sweat gently for 2 minutes. Pour in the wine, reduce by one-third, then add the stock and bring to a boil. Immediately whisk in the cooled roux, a little at a time (1). Cook the sauce at a very gentle bubble for 30 minutes, whisking it and skimming the surface every 10 minutes. Add the cream and cook until the sauce coats the back of a spoon, then whisk in the pistachio butter, a little at a time (2). As soon as it is all incorporated, stop the cooking, season the sauce, and pass it through a fine conical sieve. Serve at once, or keep it warm in a *bain-marie*, but do not allow it to boil.

Matelote Sauce

Matelote sauce goes well with pan-fried trout, whiting, monkfish tail, and many other fish. For a red matelote, use fish stock made with red wine and substitute veal stock for the fish velouté *to give the sauce a deep amber color.*

Ingredients:

1 cup Fish Stock (page 13)

⅔ cup thinly sliced button mushrooms

1¾ cups Fish Velouté (page 13)

4 tablespoons butter, or 8 tablespoons Langoustine Butter (page 24), chilled and diced

Salt and cayenne

Serves 4

*Preparation time: **5 minutes***

*Cooking time: **about 20 minutes***

Put the fish stock and mushrooms in a saucepan and cook over medium heat until half the liquid has evaporated. Add the *fish velouté* and bubble the sauce gently for 10 minutes, then pass it through a wire-mesh conical sieve into a clean pan. Off the heat, whisk in the butter, a little at a time. Season the sauce to taste with salt and cayenne.

Seaspray Sauce

This sauce has the tang of the sea. It is excellent served with braised fish, such as turbot or halibut, or with a fish pie.

Ingredients:

1½ tablespoons butter

⅓ cup chopped shallot

1 cup Fish Stock (page 13)

⅔ cup dry white wine

3 tablespoons mixed dried aromatics, ground or pulverized, consisting of equal quantities of: lavender flowers, dill seeds, lime flowers, juniper berries, coriander seeds, red pimento, lemon grass

6 sheets of dried edible seaweed (nori)

1 cup heavy cream

6 medium oysters, shucked, with their juices

Salt and freshly ground pepper

Serves 6

Preparation time: 5 minutes

Cooking time: about 25 minutes

In a saucepan, melt the butter, add the shallot, and sweat it gently for 1 minute. Pour in the fish stock and wine, then add the mixed aromatics and seaweed and cook over medium heat until the liquid has reduced by half. Add the cream together with the oysters and their juices and bubble the sauce for 5 minutes.

Transfer the contents of the saucepan to a blender and whizz for 1 minute. Pass the sauce through a wire-mesh conical sieve into a small saucepan and stand it in a *bain-marie*. Season to taste with salt and pepper and serve immediately, or keep the sauce warm in the *bain-marie* for a few minutes.

Raspberry-Scented Oyster Sauce

A sauce which subtly combines the flavors of raspberries and oysters. I poach raw oysters for just 30 seconds and serve them barely warm in a little dish with this sauce and a scattering of blanched beansprouts... Quite simply sublime!

Ingredients:

¼ cup chopped shallot
18 very ripe raspberries
1½ tablespoons sugar
¼ cup raspberry vinegar
8 medium oysters, shucked, with their juices
1 cup heavy cream
Salt and freshly ground pepper

Serves 6

Preparation time: **5 minutes**

Cooking time: **about 12 minutes**

Combine the shallot, raspberries, and sugar in a small saucepan. Cook gently for 3–4 minutes, stirring with a wooden spoon, until you have an almost jam-like purée. Add the vinegar, bubble for 3 minutes, then add the oysters and cream, and simmer gently for 5 minutes. Pour the sauce into a blender and purée for 30 seconds, then pass it through a wire-mesh conical sieve into a clean saucepan. Season to taste and serve the sauce immediately, or keep it warm for a few minutes.

Normandy Sauce

This classic sauce is wonderful not only with sole à la normande, *but with any white fish. The addition of mussel juices makes it even more delicious.*

Ingredients:

2 tablespoons butter
1½ cups thinly sliced button mushrooms
1 sprig of thyme
¼ cup White Roux, hot (page 14)
2¼ cups Fish Stock, cooled (page 13)
¼ cup mussel juices (optional)
1 cup heavy cream, mixed with 3 egg yolks
Juice of ½ lemon
Salt and freshly ground white pepper

Serves 6

Preparation time: **15 minutes**

Cooking time: **about 35 minutes**

In a saucepan, melt the butter over low heat, add the mushrooms and thyme, and sweat them for 2 minutes. Stir in the hot white roux, then pour in the cold fish stock and mussel juices, if you are using them. Mix with a small whisk and bring to a boil. Bubble the sauce gently for 20 minutes, stirring it with the whisk every 5 minutes. Add the cream and egg yolk mixture and the lemon juice, and continue to bubble the sauce gently for 10 minutes longer. Season to taste with salt and white pepper, pass the sauce through a wire-mesh conical sieve, and serve immediately.

48   Sauces for Fish and Shellfish

Hollandaise Sauce

Hollandaise sauce is one of the great classics and many other sauces derive from it. It is light, smooth, and delicate and does not like to be kept waiting; if you cannot serve it immediately, keep it covered in a warm place.

Ingredients:
¼ cup cold water
1 tablespoon white wine vinegar
½ tablespoon white peppercorns crushed
4 egg yolks
1 cup butter, freshly clarified (page 8) and cooled to tepid
Juice of ½ lemon
Salt

Serves 6 (makes about 3 cups)
Preparation time: 20 minutes
Cooking time: 12–15 minutes

Combine the water, vinegar, and pepper in a small, heavy-based, stainless steel saucepan (1). Over low heat, reduce by one-third, then let cool in a cold place.

When the liquid is cold, add the egg yolks (2) and mix thoroughly with a small whisk. Set the saucepan over a very gentle heat and whisk continuously, making sure that the whisk comes into contact with the entire bottom surface of the pan (3). Keep whisking as you gently and progressively increase the heat source; the sauce should emulsify very gradually, becoming smooth and creamy after 8–10 minutes. Do not allow the temperature of the sauce to rise above 150°F.

Take the saucepan off the heat and, whisking continuously, blend in the cooled clarified butter, a little at a time (4). Season the sauce with salt to taste.

Pass the sauce through a fine-mesh conical sieve and serve as soon as possible, stirring in the lemon juice at the last moment (5).

Noisette Sauce: ¼ cup *beurre noisette* (browned butter) added just before serving gives hollandaise sauce a delicious flavor and transforms it into a *sauce noisette*. To make the browned butter, heat some butter in a small saucepan until sizzling and nutty brown. Do not let it blacken and burn.

Hollandaise Sauce with Red Butter

I like to serve this glorious sauce with grilled lobster or a piece of pan-fried cod garnished with large shrimp and braised oyster mushrooms.

Ingredients:

1 quantity Hollandaise Sauce (page 49), made with only ⅔ cup clarified butter
1 cup Langoustine Butter (page 24)
½ tablespoon finely grated fresh ginger
¼ cup heavy cream, whipped to a floppy consistency with the juice of ½ lemon
Salt and freshly ground white pepper

Serves 6
*Preparation time: **5 minutes***
*Cooking time: **12–15 minutes***

Follow the recipe for hollandaise sauce, gradually whisking in the ⅔ cup clarified butter and the langoustine butter. Add the lemon juice specified in the hollandaise recipe, and the ginger. Very gently fold in the lemony cream, season with salt and pepper, and serve immediately.

Hollandaise Sauce with Fish Stock

This sauce is delicious with pan-fried or grilled turbot or halibut. I sometimes add a few spoons of the cooking juices from shellfish to the fish stock before reducing it, which further enhances the flavor.

Ingredients:

½ cup Fish Stock (page 13)
1 quantity Hollandaise Sauce (page 49)
1 tablespoon snipped dill
¼ cup heavy cream, whipped to soft peaks
Salt and freshly ground white pepper

Serves 6
*Preparation time: **5 minutes***
*Cooking time: **about 20 minutes***

Pour the fish stock into a small saucepan and reduce over low heat to 2 tablespoons. Whisk this reduction into the hollandaise sauce, then add the lemon juice specified in the hollandaise recipe, the dill, and the cream. Season to taste and serve at once.

Mousseline Sauce

This delicate sauce is perfect for serving with poached or steamed fish or with asparagus. When truffles are in season, I add some chopped truffle trimmings, which make the sauce even more delectable.

Ingredients:

1 quantity Hollandaise Sauce (page 49)

⅓ cup heavy cream, whipped to soft peaks

Salt and freshly ground white pepper

Serves 8

Preparation time: 5 minutes

Cooking time: 12–15 minutes

Just before serving, whisk the lemon juice specified in the hollandaise recipe and the whipped cream into the sauce. Season and serve immediately.

Maltaise Sauce

I like to serve this with crisply cooked snow peas mixed with some orange sections and asparagus. It also goes very well with poached sea trout.

Ingredients:

Juice of 1 large blood orange (preferably), or of 2 small oranges

Zest from the orange, minced, blanched, refreshed, and well drained

1 quantity Hollandaise Sauce (page 49)

Salt and freshly ground white pepper

Serves 6

Preparation time: 5 minutes

Cooking time: 12–15 minutes

Put the orange juice in a small saucepan, set over low heat, and reduce by one-third, then add the zest and take the pan off the heat. Just before serving, whisk the lemon juice specified in the hollandaise recipe into the sauce, together with the reduced orange juice and zest. Serve immediately.

Beer Sauce

This sauce is excellent with braised fish steaks, like turbot or halibut The addition of a spoonful of the braising liquid just before serving will enhance the flavor of the sauce.

Serves 4

Preparation time: **5 minutes**

Cooking time: **about 15 minutes**

Ingredients:

½ cup very finely sliced shallots

1 small bouquet garni (page 9)

4 juniper berries, crushed

1¼ cups mild beer

1 cup heavy cream

4 tablespoons butter, chilled and diced

½ tablespoon finely snipped flat-leaf parsley

Salt and freshly ground pepper

Put the shallots, bouquet garni, and juniper berries in a saucepan, pour in the beer (1), and reduce by two-thirds over medium heat (2). Add the cream (3) and bubble for 5 minutes, until the sauce will lightly coat the back of a spoon (4). If it seems too thin, cook it for a few more minutes. Pass the sauce through a conical sieve, whisk in the butter, a small piece at a time (5), and finally stir in the parsley (6). Season to taste with salt and pepper.

Beurre Blanc with Cream

Like all beurres blancs, *this must be made with a really good-quality wine vinegar and the best-quality unsalted butter. This delicate sauce is simple to make and is delicious with any poached fish. For braised fish replace the vinegar with dry sherry.*

Ingredients:

½ cup white wine vinegar

½ cup minced shallots

2 tablespoons water

¼ cup heavy cream

14 tablespoons butter, chilled and diced

Salt and freshly ground white pepper

Serves 6

Preparation time: **10 minutes**

Cooking time: **about 15 minutes**

Combine the vinegar, shallots, and water in a small, thick-bottomed saucepan and reduce the liquid over low heat by two-thirds. Add the cream and reduce again by one-third. Over low heat, whisk in the butter, a little at a time, or beat it in with a wooden spoon. It is vital to keep the sauce barely simmering at 195°F and not to let it boil during this operation. Season with salt and pepper, and serve immediately.

Beurre Rouge with Cream: You can make an unusual red version of this *beurre blanc* by substituting an equal quantity of red wine vinegar for the white wine vinegar.

Champagne Beurre Blanc

This sauce is wonderful with whole braised fish, such as John Dory or baby turbot.

Ingredients:

¼ cup champagne vinegar

½ cup minced shallots

1 sprig of thyme

½ cup brut champagne

¾ cup very finely diced button
mushrooms

1 cup butter, chilled and diced

Salt and freshly ground white pepper

Serves 6

*Preparation time: **10 minutes***

*Cooking time: **about 20 minutes***

Combine the vinegar, shallots, and thyme in a small, thick-bottomed saucepan and reduce the liquid by half over low heat. Add the champagne and mushrooms and continue to cook gently until the liquid has again reduced by half. Remove the thyme. Over low heat, whisk in the butter, a little at a time, or beat it in with a wooden spoon. It is vital to keep the sauce barely simmering at 195°F and not to let it boil during this operation. Season to taste and serve the sauce at once, or keep it hot in a *bain-marie* for a few minutes.

Cider Beurre Blanc

I adore this butter sauce served with grilled scallops, a simply poached whole sole, braised turbot, or a John Dory roasted in the oven and served whole at the table.

Ingredients:

⅓ cup cider vinegar

½ cup minced shallots

½ cup hard cider

⅓ cup peeled and finely grated apple

1 cup butter, chilled and diced

Salt and freshly ground pepper

Serves 6

*Preparation time: **10 minutes***

*Cooking time: **15 minutes***

Put the vinegar and shallot in a small, thick-bottomed saucepan, set over low heat, and reduce the liquid by half. Add the cider and grated apple and cook gently to reduce the liquid by one-third. Still over low heat, incorporate the butter, a little at a time, using a whisk or small wooden spoon. The butter sauce must not boil, but merely tremble at about 195°F. Season to taste with salt and pepper and serve immediately, or keep the sauce warm for a few minutes in a *bain-marie*.

Red-Pepper Sabayon

I serve this sabayon with poached eggs on a bed of pilaff rice, or with vegetables like cauliflower and asparagus. It is also good with grilled fish, particularly salmon. The vegetable stock can be replaced by chicken or fish stock, depending on the dish the sauce is to accompany.

Ingredients:

½ pound red bell peppers
1 cup Vegetable Stock (page 10) or
Fish Stock (page 13)
1 small sprig of thyme
4 egg yolks
4 tablespoons butter, chilled and diced
Salt and freshly ground pepper

Serves 4

Preparation time: *10 minutes*

Cooking time: *about 25 minutes*

Halve the red peppers lengthwise (left) and remove the stem, seeds, and white membranes. Coarsely chop the pepper, place in a small saucepan with the stock and thyme (1), and simmer for 15 minutes. Pour the contents of the saucepan into a blender and whizz for 1 minute. Pass the purée through a wire-mesh conical sieve into a small clean saucepan and leave until almost cold, then whisk in the egg yolks (2). Stand the pan in a *bain-marie* or over indirect heat, and whisk the *sabayon* to a ribbon consistency (3). Whisk in the butter, a little at a time (4), season the *sabayon* with salt and pepper, and serve at once.

Halve the red
peppers lengthwise

Béchamel Sauce

This is the ideal sauce for any number of dishes, such as cauliflower or endive au gratin, *macaroni and cheese made with a touch of cream and grated Gruyère or Emmenthal, a genuine* croque monsieur—*the list is endless. Like hollandaise and mayonnaise, béchamel forms the basis of innumerable other sauces.*

Ingredients:

¼ cup White Roux (page 14), cooled

2½ cups milk

Freshly grated nutmeg (optional)

Salt and freshly ground white pepper

Serves 4

Preparation time: **5 minutes**

Cooking time: **about 25 minutes**

Put the cold roux into a small, thick-bottomed saucepan. Bring the milk to a boil and pour it onto the roux, mixing and stirring with a whisk or wooden spatula. Set the pan over low heat and bring the mixture to a boil, still stirring continuously. As soon as it reaches boiling point, reduce the heat and cook at a very gentle simmer for about 20 minutes, stirring the sauce continuously (1) and making sure that the spatula or whisk scrapes across all the surfaces of the saucepan.

Season the sauce with salt, white pepper, and a very little nutmeg if you wish (2), then pass it through a conical strainer (3). You can serve it immediately or keep it warm in a *bain-marie*, in which case dot a few flakes of butter over the surface to prevent a skin from forming (4).

Béchamel sauce will keep in an airtight container in the refrigerator for a maximum of 4 days.

Béchamel Sauce forms the basis of

innumerable other sauces

Coconut and Chili Sauce

Serve this unusual spicy sauce with wide noodles or any poached firm-fleshed white fish.

Serves 8

Preparation time: *10 minutes*

Cooking time: *25 minutes*

Ingredients:

7 tablespoons butter

1 small hot red chili, seeded and minced

2 jalapeño peppers, seeded and minced

½ pound small peeled cooked shrimp (optional)

For the coconut béchamel:

2½ tablespoons butter

3 tablespoons flour

2 cups canned coconut milk

Freshly grated nutmeg

1 tablespoon soy sauce

2 garlic cloves, crushed or minced

Salt and freshly ground pepper

First make the coconut béchamel. In a small saucepan, melt the butter and stir in the flour to make a roux. Cook over low heat for 2 minutes, stirring all the time with a whisk. Add the coconut milk, bring to a boil, then immediately season with nutmeg, salt, and pepper. Cook gently for 20 minutes, stirring continuously. Remove from the heat and stir in the soy sauce and garlic.

In another small saucepan, heat the 7 tablespoons butter until it turns fragrant and golden brown. Toss in the chili peppers (1), immediately tip the mixture into the coconut béchamel, and stir until well amalgamated (2). Adjust the seasoning if necessary and stir in the shrimp at the last moment, if you are using them (3). Serve the sauce hot.

Mustard and White-Wine Sauce

This versatile sauce is perfect served with any poached or braised firm-fleshed fish.

Ingredients:

2 tablespoons butter

1 cup thinly sliced button mushrooms

½ cup minced shallots

A pinch of curry powder

1 tablespoon cognac or Armagnac

1 cup dry white wine

1 small bouquet garni (page 9)

1 cup Fish Stock (page 13)

1¼ cups heavy cream

1 teaspoon English mustard powder, dissolved in a little water

2 tablespoons wholegrain mustard

Salt and freshly ground pepper

Serves 4

Preparation time: **10 minutes**

Cooking time: **about 40 minutes**

In a saucepan, melt the butter, add the mushrooms and shallot, and sweat for 1 minute (1). Stir in the curry powder and add the cognac or Armagnac and wine (2). Bring to a boil, put in the bouquet garni, and reduce the liquid by one-third. Pour in the fish or chicken stock, and bubble for 5 minutes, then add the cream and the English mustard, and cook until the sauce is thick enough to coat the back of a spoon (3). Remove the bouquet garni, season to taste with salt and pepper, and pass the sauce through a wire-mesh conical strainer. Stir in the wholegrain mustard (4). The sauce is now ready to serve.

Mornay Sauce

You can coat a multitude of dishes with this sauce and immediately brown them lightly under a hot broiler or salamander; poached eggs, fish, vegetables, and white meats are all excellent served this way. Mixed with macaroni, mornay sauce also makes a delicious macaroni and cheese.

Ingredients:

1 quantity boiling Béchamel Sauce (page 58)

¼ cup heavy cream mixed with 3 egg yolks

1 cup grated Emmenthal, Gruyère, or Farmhouse Cheddar

Salt and freshly ground pepper

Serves 4

Preparation time: **5 minutes**

Cooking time: **about 2 minutes**

Add the cream and egg yolk mixture to a boiling béchamel and bubble for 1 minute, whisking vigorously. Remove from the heat and mix in your chosen cheese with a wooden spoon. Season the sauce with salt and pepper, and use it as you wish.

White Bordelaise or Bonnefoy Sauce

This robust, well-structured sauce makes the perfect accompaniment to fish with a rather bland flavor, such as whiting, lemon sole, or farmed trout.

Ingredients:

1¼ cups dry white wine

2 tablespoons cognac

½ cup minced shallots

1 bouquet garni (page 9)

1¾ cups Fish Velouté (page 13)

3 tablespoons butter, chilled and diced

1 tablespoon snipped tarragon leaves

Salt and freshly ground pepper

Serves 4

Preparation time: **5 minutes**

Cooking time: **about 30 minutes**

Combine the wine, cognac, shallots, and bouquet garni in a saucepan and reduce the liquid to one-third over high heat. Add the fish *velouté* and bubble the sauce gently for 20 minutes, skimming the surface whenever necessary. Pass the sauce through a wire-mesh conical sieve into a clean pan, then whisk in the butter, a little at a time. Season the sauce with salt and pepper, stir in the tarragon, and serve.

Index

Index

This edition published in 2005 by Quadrille Publishing Ltd
Alhambra House
27–31 Charing Cross Road
London WC2H 0LS

Based on material originally published in *Sauces; sweet and savoury, classic and new* by Michel Roux.

Text © 1996 & 2000 Michel Roux
Photography © 1996 Martin Brigdale
Design & layout © 2000
Quadrille Publishing Ltd

Publishing director: Anne Furniss
Art Director: Mary Evans
Art Editor: Rachel Gibson
Project editor & translator: Kate Whiteman
Editorial Assistant: Caroline Perkins
Styling: Helen Trent
Production: Rachel Wells

The right of Michel Roux to be identified as the Author of this Work has been asserted by him in accordance with the Copyright, Designs and Patents Act 1988.

Cataloguing-in-Publication Data: a catalogue record for this book is available from the British Library.

ISBN 1 84400 186 5

Printed in China through World Print Ltd.